KU-488-124

Marjorie Lampard

compiler

The Calorie Counter

MAYFLOWER
GRANADA PUBLISHING
London Toronto Sydney New York

Published by Granada Publishing Limited
in Mayflower Books 1974
Reprinted 1975, 1976 (twice), 1977, 1978 (twice), 1979

ISBN 0 583 12309 0

Copyright © Mayflower Books Ltd 1974

Granada Publishing Limited
Frogmore, St Albans, Herts AL2 2NF
and
3 Upper James Street, London W1R 4BP
1221 Avenue of the Americas, New York, NY 10020, USA
117 York Street, Sydney, NSW 2000, Australia
100 Skyway Avenue, Toronto, Ontario, Canada M9W 3A6
110 Northpark Centre, 2193 Johannesburg, South Africa
CML Centre, Queen & Wyndham, Auckland 1, New Zealand

Made and printed in Great Britain by
Richard Clay (The Chaucer Press) Ltd
Bungay, Suffolk
Set in Monotype Times

This book is sold subject to the condition that it
shall not, by way of trade or otherwise, be lent,
re-sold, hired out or otherwise circulated
without the publisher's prior consent in any
form of binding or cover other than that in
which it is published and without a similar
condition including this condition being imposed
on the subsequent purchaser.

Granada Publishing ®

Note

The figures given in *The Calorie Counter* have been calculated from *The Composition of Foods*, Medical Research Council SRS 297, by R. A. McCance and E. M. Widdowson, issued by Her Majesty's Stationery Office; and from statistics prepared by the United States Department of Agriculture and the United States Society of Actuaries.

Contents

INTRODUCTION

The diet that succeeds is the one that lasts. And the reason why it lasts is that it is interesting – so interesting, in fact, that one can keep to it without constantly being reminded that it *is* a diet. Anyone who decided – unwisely – to lose weight by eating nothing but grapefruit and hard-boiled eggs, for example, would almost certainly get rid of some excess pounds, but they would also find, after about a week, that they began to long for foods with different flavours and textures. And, as every would-be dieter knows with sorrow, once you begin to dwell on the thought of what it would be like to eat just one potato in its jacket, or to see visions of apple pie and cream, your current diet is on its way out.

The solution is to follow a diet that is healthy, simple and, above all, varied – in fact, as un-dietlike as possible. The one that fulfils all these requirements for success is based on a calorie count. This is both easy and interesting to calculate, and its strongest point is that it enables you to eat the foods you enjoy.

What is a calorie?

'Calorie' is the name given by both physicists and nutritionists to a small measure of heat. The body, through the digestive process, converts food into fuel, which it then proceeds to burn up in order to create energy. You are unlikely to become overweight if the number of calories provided by what you eat and drink are balanced by the amount of energy which you use up during a day. Incidentally, for the body's food-into-heat-into-energy process, a day means twenty-four hours. You will notice the expenditure of energy when you run upstairs or play a game of tennis, for example, but even when you are completely relaxed or fast asleep, your body is continuously using energy to keep your heart pumping and your lungs working – in short, to keep you alive.

How many calories?

Suppose that your body has more calories than it wants for the amount of energy it has to produce: suppose, to put the question in a different way, that you are eating too much? Your body will store the surplus calories in the form of fat, and in time you will feel – and see – that you need to diet.

It is a shock, but a useful one, to realize that one pound of excess fat is equivalent to *3,500 calories*. They could be accumulated in one week by over-eating to the extent of 500 calories each day, or in a month, by over-eating to the order of 100 calories per day. When you decide to bring your weight down to its right level for your health and looks you can do it by reducing your normal daily calorie requirement by as much as a half. Your body will make up the deficit from the store of fat.

However, it is obviously better in every way to prevent a build-up of excess calories, rather than to have to go to the trouble of demolishing it. The way to prevent it is to keep a steady balance between the total number of calories which your food provides and the energy you expend every twenty-four hours. If your daily calorie requirement is 2,000 and the food you eat provides this 2,000 the weight of your body will remain at its right level for health.

In order to achieve this pleasant state of affairs, you need three pieces of information:

1. What is a healthy weight for someone of your height and build?
2. How many calories do you need each day?
3. How many calories are in the foods you eat and the liquids you drink?

10

1. Correct weight

There are no hard-and-fast rules about the relationship between the weight of a human body and its height and general structure. However, the charts on pages 15 and 16 provides you with a useful working guide. Remember, however, that it only gives you an approximate target weight. Its main purpose is to help you to work out whether you really are at all over-weight, or whether you simply feel that you would be happier if you were slimmer.

2. Calorie requirement

This varies from one individual to another. For one thing, of course, it depends upon build and height, but other factors help to determine it, too:

Sex. Men, on the whole, use up more calories in the expenditure of energy during a day than women do. For a man, the daily calorie requirement is approximately 2,750, and for a woman approximately 2,200. (It is important to stress the word 'approximately' there.)

Age. Older people need less calories than young ones. The reduction in the requirement begins at about the age of 25.

Way of life. This means particularly 'way of work'. A man who does a job requiring continuous physical effort will need more calories than one who works mainly at a desk. A woman who spends a large part of her leisure in walking or gardening is most likely to require more calories than one whose chief relaxation is reading or knitting, for example.

Other less-defined factors. Individual calorie requirement is influenced, too, by factors which are still being researched. For example, two people of the same height and general build will not necessarily need the same daily intake of calories. Another instance: a person who regularly takes in more than his or her calorie requirement will burn up the excess and not gain a store of surplus fat, while another individual will absorb less calories than the basic requirement according to his or her height and build and yet still be over-weight.

Nutritionists are still discovering why these and other differences should be so: why it is that some people should be exceptions to the dietary 'rules'. One explanation is that in some of us the whole process of converting food into heat and then into energy is simply more efficient than it is in others: that the body's own apparatus for balancing intake of food and output of energy varies in accuracy from one individual to another.

One thing, however, is beyond question: you may not think that you over-eat, but if you *do* eat more than you need, it is too much. Too much food = too many calories = stored fat. Count your calories and stay slim and well.

3. *Counting the calories*

On pages 17–33 there is a comprehensive list of foods and drinks, arranged in alphabetical order, giving both the calorie value of an average serving and the number of calories per ounce.

Following the Calorie Counter, on page 39 there begins a selection of low-calorie recipes, for Breakfasts, Starters, Main Meals, Snacks, Salads and Puddings. All the dishes have been expertly worked out so that they provide a balanced selection of essential nutrients – proteins, vitamins and minerals – as well as keeping the total number of calories down.

When you are working out your own calorie-controlled meals, be sure that you include, every day, foods from these four main groups:

1. Milk and milk products, including cheese and yogurt
2. Meat, poultry, fish and eggs
3. Fruit (especially citrus and soft fruits), vegetables and salads
4. Bread, white or brown – up to 3 ounces each day

Finally, whether you are over-weight or under-weight, consult your doctor before you begin to diet. He can advise you about the amount of weight which you could lose (or gain) with advantage to your general health, and about the approximate number of calories which you need each day.

WHAT SHOULD YOU WEIGH?

(The weights in the chart below only indicate a target to aim at. Each of them is nothing more than an approximation: it is not something to be achieved at all costs.)

WOMEN*			
Height in shoes with 2-inch heels	Small frame	Medium frame	Large frame
ft. in.	st. lb.	st. lb.	st. lb.
4 10	6 8	6 12	7 6
4 11	6 10	7 0	7 8
5 0	6 12	7 3	7 11
5 1	7 1	7 6	8 0
5 2	7 4	7 9	8 3
5 3	7 7	7 12	8 6
5 4	7 10	8 1	8 9
5 5	7 13	8 4	8 13
5 6	8 2	8 8	9 3
5 7	8 8	8 12	9 7
5 8	8 10	9 2	9 11
5 9	9 0	9 6	10 1
5 10	9 4	9 10	10 5
5 11	9 8	10 0	10 9
6 0	9 12	10 4	10 13

* For girls aged 18–25, subtract 1lb. for each year under 25.

Height in shoes with 1-inch heels	Small frame	Medium frame	Large frame
ft. in.	st. lb.	st. lb.	st. lb.
5 2	8 3	8 6	9 0
5 3	8 3	8 9	9 3
5 4	8 6	8 12	9 6
5 5	8 9	9 1	9 9
5 6	8 12	9 4	9 12
5 7	9 2	9 8	10 2
5 8	9 6	9 12	10 7
5 9	9 10	10 2	10 11
5 10	10 0	10 6	11 1
5 11	10 4	10 10	11 5
6 0	10 8	11 0	11 10
6 1	10 12	11 4	12 0
6 2	11 2	11 8	12 5
6 3	11 6	11 13	12 10
6 4	11 10	12 4	13 0

THE CALORIE COUNTER

The idea of the size of an 'average serving' varies, of course, from one person to another. If you feel that you are not losing as much weight as you expected by counting calories, check the weight of the portions you are eating. Divide the figure given in the first column, headed *Calories in an average serving*, by the figure in the second column, *Calories per ounce*. The result will be the size (in ounces) of the particular portion. If you then weigh the portion which you would normally eat, and find that it is larger than the average serving, you have discovered why your weight loss is slower than you had hoped. The solution, of course, is simple: smaller portions, less calories, less weight.

* against foods in the following list means that they are 'empty calories': in other words, they contain only very small amounts of essential nutrients, such as proteins and vitamins, and so are best avoided in a calorie-controlled diet.
† against foods in the list means that there is a recipe for them in the next section of the book.

A	Calories	
	Per average serving	Per ounce
Alcoholic beverages – see 'Beer', 'Wine', 'Spirits', 'Liqueurs' and 'Cocktails'		
All Bran – Kellogg's	90	88
Almonds – without shells	—	170
Almonds – weighed with shells	—	63
Apple crumble (½ cup)*	355	63
Apple dumpling – made with short pastry*	340	57
Apple pie – single crust, short pastry*	325	54

A continued

	Calories	
	Per average serving	Per ounce
Apple pudding – made with suet pastry*	410	68
Apple snow†	30	9
Apples – baked, weighed with skin	45	9
Apples – eating, weighed with skin and core	50	10
Apples – stewed without sugar	35	9
Apricots – canned in syrup	120	30
Apricots – dried, raw	—	52
Apricots – dried, stewed without sugar	70	17
Apricots – fresh, stewed without sugar	25	6
Apricots – fresh, weighed with stone	30	7
Arrowroot	—	101
Artichokes – globe, weighed as served	15	2
Artichokes – Jerusalem, boiled	20	5
Asparagus – boiled, weighed as served	15	3
Asparagus soup†	20	3
Avocado	100	25

B

Bacon – back, fried (2 rashers or 2 oz.)	340	169
Bacon – collar, fried (1 rasher or 1½ oz.)	185	124
Bacon – gammon, fried (1 rasher or 2 oz.)	250	126
Bacon – streaky, fried (4 rashers or 2 oz.)	300	149
Banana custard	150	29
Bananas – peeled (1 large)	80	22
Bananas – weighed with skin (1 large)	80	13
Barcelona nuts	—	189
Barcelona nuts – weighed with shells	—	117
Barley – pearl, raw	—	102
Barley – pearl, boiled	—	34
Beans – baked	80	26
Beans – broad, boiled	35	12
Beans – butter and haricot, raw	—	76
Beans – butter and haricot, boiled	80	26
Beans – runner, French, raw	—	4
Beans – runner, French, boiled	10	2
Beef – corned	265	66
Beef – sirloin, roast, lean only	255	64
Beef – sirloin, roast, lean and fat	235	109
Beef – steak, fried	325	86

	Calories	
	Per average serving	Per ounce
Beef – steak, grilled	325	78
Beef – steak, stewed	245	58
Beef – steak and kidney pie with flaky pastry	515	86
Beefsteak pudding, with suet pastry	445	74
Beef stew, with vegetables	240	40
Beef – topside, boiled	245	61
Beef – topside, roast, lean only	285	71
Beef – topside, roast, lean and fat	365	91
Beer – bitter, draught	100	9
Beer – brown ale, bottled	100	8
Beer – mild, draught	90	7
Beer – pale ale, bottled	100	9
Beer – stout, bottled	110	10
Beer – stout, extra	120	11
Beetroot – boiled	50	13
Bemax	25	105
Biscuits – digestive	135	137
Biscuits – sweet, mixed	155	158
Biscuits – water	65	127
Blackberries – raw	30	8
Blackberries – stewed without sugar	30	6
Blancmange	135	34
Bloaters – grilled, weighed with skin and bones	325	54
Boiled sweets	100	93
Bone and vegetable broth	130	18
Bournvita	50	105
Bovril	—	23
Brain – calf, boiled	85	29
Brazil nuts	—	183
Brazil nuts – weighed with shells	—	82
Bread – currant	70	71
Bread – Hovis	65	67
Bread – malt	70	71
Bread – procea	70	72
Bread – wheatmeal	70	68
Bread – white	70	70
Bread – fried, white	162	162
Bread – toasted, white	185	85
Bread – wholemeal	67	65
Bread and butter pudding	200	46
Breadcrumbs, white, dried	—	101
Bread sauce	30	32

B continued

	Calories	
	Per average serving	Per ounce
Bream – red, steamed, weighed with bones	100	17
Brill – steamed, weighed with bones	130	22
Broccoli tops – boiled	15	4
Brown sauce – bottled	30	28
Brown sauce – home-made (Espagnole)	60	33
Brussels sprouts – raw	—	9
Brussels sprouts – boiled	20	5
Buck rarebit	350	81
Butter	110	226
Butterscotch	—	116

C

Cabbage – red, raw	10	6
Cabbage – Savoy, boiled	15	3
Cabbage – spring, boiled	10	2
Cabbage – winter, raw	15	7
Cabbage – winter, boiled	15	3
Cakes – cherry*	260	129
Cakes – chocolate*	280	141
Cakes – coconut*	150	126
Cakes – currant*	240	119
Cakes – Dundee*	220	110
Cakes – gingerbread*	220	108
Cakes – rock*	240	119
Cakes – sponge*	180	87
Cakes – Victoria sandwich*	170	134
Carrots – raw	10	6
Carrots – boiled	20	5
Catfish – fried	350	57
Catfish – fried, weighed with bones	350	53
Catfish – steamed	200	34
Catfish – steamed, weighed with bones	200	28
Cauliflower – raw	15	7
Cauliflower – boiled	15	3
Celeriac – boiled	15	4
Celery – raw	5	3
Celery – boiled	5	1
Cheese – Camembert	90	88
Cheese – Cheddar	120	120
Cheese – Cheshire	110	110
Cheese – cream	230	232

20

	Calories Per average serving	Per ounce
Cheese – Danish blue	103	100
Cheese – Edam	88	90
Cheese – Gorgonzola	112	110
Cheese – Gouda	96	100
Cheese – Gruyère	132	130
Cheese – Parmesan	118	120
Cheese – processed	106	100
Cheese – St. Ivel	108	100
Cheese – Stilton	135	130
Cheese – Wensleydale	115	110
Cheese sauce	52	200
Cherries	13	45
Cherries – weighed with stones	11	45
Cherries – stewed without sugar	10	45
Cherries – glacé	60	—
Cocktails – Bloody Mary	140	—
Cocktails – champagne	125	—
Cocktails – gin fizz	165	—
Cocktails – martini	135	—
Cocktails – Tom Collins	165	—
Cocktails – whisky sour	140	—
Cocoa powder	40	128
Cod – fried skinned fillets	250	40
Cod – fried with bones and skin	250	36
Cod – grilled	270	45
Cod – grilled, weighed with bones and skin	270	39
Cod – steamed	140	23
Cod – steamed, weighed with bones and skin	140	18
Cod-liver oil	—	264
Cod roe – fried	240	59
Cod roe – baked in vinegar	140	34
Coffee – infusion of	5	1
Coffee – Irish*	250	60
Coffee and chicory essence	60	63
Compound cooking fat	—	262
Cornflakes – Kellogg's	100	104
Cornflour	—	100
Crab – boiled	140	36
Crab – boiled, weighed with shells	140	7
Cranberries	—	4
Cream – double	130	131
Cream – single	60	62

C continued

	Calories	
	Per average serving	Per ounce
Cucumber – raw	5	3
Currants – black, stewed without sugar	20	6
Currants – dried	—	69
Currants – red, stewed without sugar	15	4
Currants – white, stewed without sugar	20	6
Curry powder	—	67
Custard – egg, sauce	100	34
Custard – egg, baked	150	32
Custard powder	—	100
Custard sauce made with powder	100	33
Custard tart	160	82

D

Dabs – fried	280	71
Damsons – raw	40	11
Damsons – stewed without sugar, weighed with stones	40	8
Dates	140	70
Dates – weighed with stones	140	61
Dogfish – fried	375	94
Doughnuts*	200	101
Dripping – beef	—	262
Duck – roast	350	89
Duck – roast, weighed with bone	350	48
Dumpling – suet	120	59

E

Eccles cakes*	300	147
Eels – weighed with skin and bones	120	33
Eggs – whole	90	46
Eggs – white	—	11
Eggs – yolk	—	99
Eggs – fried	135	68
Eggs – poached	90	45
Eggs – scotch	300	75
Eggs – scrambled	160	79
Egg sauce	160	42
Energen rolls	55	111

F	Calories Per average serving	Per ounce
Farex	—	97
Figs – dried, raw	60	61
Figs – dried, stewed without syrup	—	30
Figs – green	25	12
Fish – see individual names		
Fish paste	—	49
Flour – white	—	100
Flour – wholemeal	—	95
Fruit gums	—	49
Fruit jelly†	120	20
Fruit pudding – made with mixed dried fruit and steamed*	360	92
Fruit salad – canned in syrup	80	20

G		
Ginger – ground	—	74
Ginger biscuits	125	127
Gingerbread	220	108
Goose – roast	370	92
Goose – roast, weighed with bone	370	53
Gooseberries – raw	—	5–10
Gooseberries – stewed without sugar	15	4
Gooseberry pie	300	51
Grapefruit – segments	25	6
Grapefruit – weighed in skin	25	3
Grapefruit squash – undiluted	40	40
Grapenuts	100	102
Grapes – black and white	60	17
Grapes – weighed whole	60	15
Greengages – raw	—	14
Greengages – stewed without sugar and weighed with stones	45	11
Grouse – roast	200	49
Grouse – roast, weighed with bone	200	32
Guinea fowl – roast	230	60
Guinea fowl – roast, weighed with bone	230	32

H		
Haddock – fried fillets	300	50
Haddock – fried, weighed with bones	300	46
Haddock – smoked, steamed fillets	170	28

	Calories	
	Per average serving	Per ounce
Haddock – smoked, steamed, weighed with bones and skin	170	18
Haddock – steamed, weighed with bones and skin	170	21
Haddock fillets – steamed	170	28
Hake – fried	350	58
Hake – fried, weighed with bones and skin	350	55
Hake – steamed	180	30
Hake – steamed, weighed with bones and skin	180	24
Halibut – steamed	220	37
Halibut – steamed, weighed with bones and skin	220	28
Ham – boiled, lean only	250	62
Ham – boiled, lean and fat	400	123
Hare – roast or stewed	220	55
Hare – roast or stewed, weighed with bones	220	37
Heart – sheep, roast	200	68
Herring – fried in oatmeal, weighed with bones	360	59
Herring – baked in vinegar, weighed with bones	300	50
Herring roe – fried	295	74
Honey	80	82
Horlick's malted milk	85	113
Horseradish – raw	—	3
Hot pot	300	35

I

Ice-cream – vanilla	120	56
Imperial biscuits	130	133
Irish stew	350	42

J

Jam*	70	73
Jam omelette	390	78
Jam roll – baked*	460	115
Jam tarts*	115	112
Jelly – made-up dish	100	23
Jelly – milk	120	31
Jelly – packet	—	73

| J continued | Calories | |
	Per average serving	Per ounce
John Dory – steamed	160	27
John Dory – steamed, weighed with bones and skin	160	17
K		
Special 'K'	100	105
Kedgeree	160	43
Kidney – ox, stewed	180	45
Kidney – sheep, fried	180	57
Kidney ragoût†	200	—
Kippers – baked	240	57
Kippers – baked, weighed with bones and skin	240	43
L		
Lamb and tomato casserole†	460	—
Lard	—	262
Leeks – raw	30	9
Leeks – boiled	30	7
Lemons – whole	—	4
Lemon curd	90	86
Lemon curd tarts	150	125
Lemon juice	2	2
Lemon sole – steamed	155	26
Lemon sole – steamed, weighed with bones and skin	155	18
Lemon sole – fried	360	62
Lemon sole – fried, weighed with bones and skin	360	49
Lemon squash – undiluted	35	36
Lemonade	60	6
Lentils – raw	30	9
Lentils – boiled	30	7
Lentil soup	150	29
Lettuce	15	3
Lime juice cordial – undiluted	30	32
Ling – fried	350	59
Ling – fried, weighed with bones and skin	350	52
Ling – steamed	160	28
Ling – steamed, weighed with bones and skin	160	21
Liqueurs – Anisette	75	—

	Calories Per average serving	Per ounce
Liqueurs – Benedictine	75	—
Liqueurs – Brandy	75	—
Liqueurs – Chartreuse	75	—
Liqueurs – Cherry Brandy	90	—
Liqueurs – Cherry Heering*	60	—
Liqueurs – Crème de Cacao	75	—
Liqueurs – Crème de Menthe	90	—
Liqueurs – Curaçao	70	—
Liqueurs – Drambuie	65	—
Liqueurs – Kümmel	70	—
Liquorice allsorts*	—	90
Liver – calf, fried	290	74
Liver – ox, fried	320	81
Lobster – boiled	125	34
Lobster – boiled, weighed with shell	125	12
Loganberries	20	5
Loganberries – stewed without sugar	20	4
Loganberries – canned in syrup	120	29
Lucozade*	80	19
Luncheon meat – canned	380	95

M

	Per average serving	Per ounce
Macaroni – raw	200	102
Macaroni – boiled	200	32
Macaroni cheese	400	59
Mackerel – fried	300	53
Mackerel – fried, weighed with bones and skin	300	39
Mandarin oranges – canned	80	18
Margarine	65	226
Marmalade	75	74
Marmite	—	2
Marrow – boiled	10	2
Mars bar*	250	127
Meat paste	—	61
Melon	50	7
Melon – weighed with skin	50	4
Milk – fresh, whole	380	19
Milk – fresh, skimmed	200	10
Milk – condensed, whole, sweetened	50	100
Milk – condensed, whole, unsweetened	25	44
Milk – condensed, skimmed, sweetened	35	76
Milk – dried, whole	75	150

	Calories	
	Per average serving	*Per ounce*
Milk – dried, skimmed	45	93
Milk – human	—	19
Milk – Ostermilk No. 1	65	129
Mincemeat	40	37
Mince pies*	120	111
Monkfish – steamed	300	48
Monkfish – steamed, weighed with bones and skin	300	39
Mulberries	40	10
Mullet – red and grey, steamed	220	36
Mullet – red and grey, steamed, weighed with bones and skin	220	23
Mushrooms – raw	—	2
Mushrooms – fried	120	62
Mussels – boiled	75	25
Mussels – boiled, weighed with shells	75	7
Mustard	—	132
Mustard and cress	6	3
Mutton – leg, boiled	280	74
Mutton – leg, roast	320	83
Mutton – scrag and neck, stewed	360	92
Mutton – scrag and neck, stewed, weighed with bone	360	69
Mutton chop – grilled, lean only	230	77
Mutton chop – grilled, weighed with fat and bone	230	36
Mutton chop – grilled, lean and fat	450	142
Mutton chop – grilled, lean and fat weighed with bone	450	108

N

Nectarines	25	14
Nectarines – weighed with stones	25	13
Nescafé (not reconstituted)	—	25
Normandy chicken†	400	—
Nuts – see individual names	—	—

O

Oatmeal – raw	—	115
Oatmeal – porridge	70	13
Olive oil*	—	264
Olives – in brine	100	30

	Calories	
	Per average serving	Per ounce
Olives – in brine, weighed with stones	100	24
Omelette, plain	225	57
Onions – raw	—	7
Onion sauce	100	25
Oranges	50	10
Oranges – weighed with skin and pips	50	8
Orange cake	260	132
Orange cake – iced	260	133
Orange juice	30	11
Orange squash, undiluted	40	39
Ovaltine	25	109
Oxo cubes	—	33
Oysters – raw	40	14
Oysters – raw, weighed with shells	40	2

P

Pancakes	175	85
Parsley	—	6
Parsnips – boiled	60	16
Partridge – roast	250	60
Partridge – roast, weighed with bone	250	36
Passion fruit	40	10
Passion fruit – weighed with skin	40	4
Pastry – flaky*	250	167
Pastry – short crust*	275	157
Peaches – canned in syrup	80	19
Peaches – dried, raw	—	61
Peaches – dried, stewed without sugar	80	20
Peaches – fresh	40	11
Peaches – fresh, weighed with stones	40	9
Peanuts	—	171
Peanuts – weighed with shells	100	118
Pears – eating	50	12
Pears – eating, weighed with skin and core	50	8
Pears – stewed without sugar	30	8
Pears – canned in syrup	80	18
Peas – canned	70	24
Peas – dried, raw	—	78
Peas – dried, boiled	85	28
Peas – fresh, raw	—	18
Peas – fresh, boiled	40	14
Peppermints	—	111

P continued	Calories	
	Per average serving	*Per ounce*
Pheasant – roast	250	61
Pheasant – roast, weighed with bone	250	38
Pigeon – boiled	250	62
Pigeon – boiled, weighed with bone	250	27
Pigeon – roast	270	66
Pigeon – roast, weighed with bone	270	29
Pilchards – canned, fish only	100	54
Pilchards – canned, fish with oil	120	63
Pineapple – canned in syrup	80	18
Pineapple – fresh	50	13
Pineapple juice	60	15
Plaice – fried	395	66
Plaice – fried, weighed with bones and skin	395	40
Plaice – steamed	155	26
Plaice – steamed, weighed with bones and skin	155	14
Plums – cooking, raw	—	7
Plums – stewed without sugar	25	6
Plums – Victoria dessert	50	11
Plums – Victoria dessert, weighed with stones	50	10
Plum pie	310	52
Pork – leg, roast	360	90
Pork – loin, roast, lean only	320	81
Pork – loin, roast, lean and fat	500	129
Pork chop – grilled, lean only	360	92
Pork chop – grilled, lean only, weighed with bone	360	38
Pork chop – grilled, lean and fat	620	155
Pork chop – grilled, lean and fat, weighed with bone	620	128
Potatoes – new, boiled	105	21
Potatoes – old, baked in skins	120	30
Potatoes – old, baked in skins, weighed with skins	120	24
Potatoes – old, boiled	120	23
Potatoes – old, chips	275	68
Potatoes – old, mashed	120	34
Potatoes – old, roast	140	30
Potato crisps	150	159
Potato soup	125	26
Prawns	60	30
Prawns – weighed with shells	60	11

P continued

	Calories	
	Per average serving	Per ounce
Prunes – dried, raw	—	46
Prunes – dried, raw, weighed with stones	—	38
Prunes – stewed without sugar, weighed with stones	80	19
Puffed wheat	100	102
Pumpkin – raw	—	24

Q

Queen cakes*	250	129
Quinces	20	7

R

Rabbit – stewed	200	51
Rabbit – stewed, weighed with bone	200	26
Radishes	10	4
Raisins – dried	—	70
Raspberries	25	7
Raspberries – stewed without sugar	25	7
Rhubarb – stewed without sugar	—	1
Ribena	65	65
Rice – raw	200	102
Rice – boiled	200	35
Rice Krispies	100	100
Ryvita	100	98

S

Sago	—	101
Salad cream – Heinz	100	111
Salmon – canned	160	39
Salmon – fresh, steamed	225	57
Salmon – fresh, steamed, weighed with bones	225	46
Salmon mousse*	140	—
Sardines – canned	160	84
Sausage – beef, fried	160	81
Sausage – black	80	81
Sausage – breakfast	160	82
Sausage – pork, fried	180	93
Sausage roll – flaky pastry*	280	142

	Calories	
	Per average serving	Per ounce
Sausage roll – short pastry*	270	134
Scallops – steamed	120	30
Scones	100	105
Semolina	—	100
Semolina pudding	160	37
Shepherd's pie	250	32
Shortbread	100	148
Shredded wheat	100	103
Shrimps	65	32
Shrimps – weighed with shells	65	11
Skate – fried	420	69
Skate – fried, weighed with bones	420	57
Sole – fried	400	78
Sole – fried, weighed with bones	400	68
Sole – steamed	155	24
Sole – steamed, weighed with bones	155	14
Soya flour	—	123
Spaghetti*	210	104
Spaghetti – canned in tomato sauce – Heinz	100	17
Spinach – boiled	30	7
Spirits – all those of 70% proof, including whisky, gin, rum, vodka	125	63
Sponge cake*	180	87
Sprats – fried	500	126
Sprats – fried, weighed with bones and heads	500	111
Spring greens – boiled	15	3
Steak and kidney pie	520	86
Strawberries	25	7
Suet	—	262
Suet pudding – plain	420	105
Suet pudding – with raisins	400	100
Sugar – Demerara	100	112
Sugar – white	100	112
Sultanas – dried	—	71
Swedes – boiled	20	5
Sweetbreads – stewed	4	51
Sweet potatoes – boiled	90	23
Syrup – golden	80	84
Syrup – sponge pudding*	400	104

T	Calories Per average serving	Per ounce
Tangerines	40	10
Tangerines – weighed with skin and pips	40	7
Tapioca	—	102
Tapioca pudding	160	37
Toad-in-the-hole	480	82
Toffees – mixed*	—	123
Tomatoes	20	4
Tomato soup, iced†	25	3
Tongue – ox, stewed	340	85
Treacle – black	70	73
Treacle tart*	400	107
Trifle	170	43
Tripe – stewed	120	29
Trout – steamed	230	38
Trout – steamed, weighed with bones and skin	230	25
Turbot – steamed	160	28
Turbot – steamed, weighed with bones and skin	160	19
Turkey – roast	225	56
Turkey – roast, weighed with bone	225	34
Turnip – boiled	10	3
V		
Veal – cutlet, fried	240	61
Veal – fillet, roast	240	66
Vegetable soup – canned, Heinz	75	12
Venison – roast	225	56
Vermouth – dry	110	—
Vermouth – sweet	175	—
Virol	—	99
Vita-weat	100	120
W		
Walnuts	—	156
Walnuts – weighed with shells	—	100
Watercress	10	4
Weetabix	100	100
Welsh cheese cakes	200	139
Welsh rarebit	300	102
Whelks	50	26

	Calories Per average serving	Per ounce
Whelks – weighed with shells	50	4
Whitebait – fried	300	152
White sauce – savoury	160	41
White sauce – sweet	190	47
Whiting – fried	330	55
Whiting – fried, weighed with bones and skin	330	49
Whiting – steamed	155	26
Whiting – steamed, weighed with bones and skin	155	17
Wines – Champagne	75	21
Wines – dry red wines, including Beaujolais, burgundy, claret and Chianti	70	20
Wines – dry white wines, including Chablis, Moselle and Rhine wines	65	18
Wines – madeira	110	38
Wines – port	130	44
Wines – sherry, dry	100	33
Wines – sherry, sweet	110	38
Wines – sweet white wines, including Graves and Sauternes	90	25
Winkles – boiled	45	21
Winkles – boiled, weighed with shells	45	4
Witch – fried	395	66
Witch – fried, weighed with bones and skin	395	56
Witch – steamed	150	25
Witch – steamed, weighed with bones and skin	150	15

Y

Yogurt – fruit	160	32
Yogurt – plain	75	25
Yorkshire pudding	240	63

Low-calorie Foods

Compared with many foods, the ones listed below contain comparatively few calories – less than 10 calories an ounce. Although they cannot be eaten indiscriminately, generous servings may be eaten by the slimmer on a calorie-controlled diet. Include some foods from this list of low-calorie foods to make slimming meals more satisfying.

Note: Calorific values for fruit and vegetables are based on the *raw* food unless stated otherwise.
For fruit, the calorific values for the cooked food are given for stewing *without* sugar.

Fruit	*Calories per ounce*
Apricots – fresh or stewed	6–7
Blackberries – fresh or stewed	6–8
Cranberries	4
Currants – red, black or white (not dried), fresh or stewed	4–8
Damsons	8–11
Gooseberries – fresh or stewed	4–10
Grapefruit	6
Lemons	4
Loganberries	5
Melon	6–7
Plums – stewed 'cookers'	6
Raspberries	7
Rhubarb – stewed	1
Strawberries	7

Vegetables and Salads	
Artichokes – boiled	2–5
Asparagus – boiled	3
Beans – French, runner, kidney, boiled	2
Broccoli – boiled	4
Brussels sprouts – boiled	5
Cabbage – boiled	3
Cabbage – raw	7
Carrots – boiled	5
Cauliflower – boiled	3
Cauliflower – raw	7
Celery raw	3
Chicory	3
Cucumber	3
Endive	3
Green peppers	4
Leeks – boiled	7

Vegetables and Salads continued

	Calories per ounce
Lettuce	3
Mustard and cress	3
Onions – boiled not fried	10
Onions – raw	7
Radishes	4
Spinach – boiled	7
Swedes and turnips – boiled	5
Tomatoes	4
Watercress	4

Flavourings and Seasonings

Capers	3
Chives	3
Curry powder	3
Garlic	7–10
Herbs – including parsley, marjoram, sage, rosemary	4 7
Horseradish sauce	5
Mustard – prepared	10
Pepper and salt	0
Spices – including cinnamon, cloves, ginger, nutmeg	0
Vinegar	2
Worcestershire sauce	10

Beverages

Consommé	1
Coffee – no milk or sugar	1
Tea – no milk or sugar	1

A QUICK COUNT

Calorie counting in units of 50 or 100 calories is both quick and easy. The amounts of food in the two sections which follow are based on *average* calorie values, and they will be a useful guide when you are working out the approximate value in calories of a meal or a snack.

50-calorie portions

1 large tomato
2 cucumbers
1 onion
1 artichoke
1 pat of butter
1 pat of margarine
1 tangerine
1 large peach
1 tablespoon double cream
1 tablespoon maple syrup
1 tablespoon sugar
3 French fries
3 small carrots
6 anchovy fillets

4 potato crisps
6 Polo mints
1 cup pickled beetroot
2 Brazil nuts
1 slice French bread
2 sticks chewing gum
2 marshmallows
1 cup tomato juice
2 digestive biscuits
2 cups green beans
2 cups cauliflower
1 cup cooked broccoli
4 small shrimps
1 fish finger

100-calorie portions

1 scrambled egg
1 oz. roast lamb
1 oz. roast beef
1 oz. roast pork
2 ounces roast chicken
1 soft bread roll
1 scone
1 baked potato
½ cup mashed potato
⅔ cup rice
1 large apple

2 oz. kidney, fried
2 oz. fried white fish
3 oz. steamed white fish
1 oz. pork sausage
1½ oz. fatty fish – e.g.
   herring or sardine
1 large banana
1 whole small grapefruit
1 pear
1 cup grapes
1 cup raspberries

$\frac{1}{4}$ pint milk
3 oz. cottage cheese
1 oz. breakfast cereal – not
   sugar-frosted

$\frac{1}{2}$ oz. chocolate
1 oz. fruit cake
1 tablespoon mayonnaise

LOW-CALORIE RECIPES

To give you an idea of how interesting and delicious a low-calorie diet can be, here are suggestions for three menus composed from the recipes that follow:

MENU 1

Breakfast

½ grapefruit
Grilled bacon with mushrooms
Slice starch-reduced crispbread
Cup of tea or coffee

Lunch (or supper) snack

Cheese and pineapple salad

Main meal of the day

Asparagus soup
Lamb and tomato casserole
Portion of spinach
Apple Snow

Total calories for 1 person: 731

MENU 2

Breakfast

Stewed prunes
Scrambled egg
Toast made with slice starch-reduced bread
Cup of tea or coffee

Lunch (or supper) snack
Crab and celery salad

Main meal of the day
Brown onion soup
Mexican Chicken
Green salad
Pear Meringue

Total calories for 1 person: 893

MENU 3

Breakfast
Yogurt
Banana and corn flakes
Cup of tea or coffee

Lunch (or supper) snack
Tomato and chicken deckers

Main meal of the day
Chicken and herb soup
Slimmers' Boeuf Stroganoff
Boiled celery
Coffee cream

Total calories for 1 person: 814

BREAKFASTS

Breakfast is an essential start to every day – it not only makes you feel good but keeps you going until lunch time, so you are not tempted to nibble in between meals. Forget the idea that it takes a long time to have a cooked breakfast – it doesn't, it can all be prepared the night before. So all you have to do while waiting for the kettle to boil is to pop the pan on the cooker or under the grill. With breakfast, have a piece of starch-reduced bread or a roll with butter from the day's allowance and remember, no sugar in tea or coffee, but you can have some milk from your daily ½ pint.

Orange juice	1 oz. = 11 calories
Grilled bacon	1 oz. = 157 calories
and tomato	1 oz. = 20 calories
Yogurt	5 oz. carton = 75 calories
Fresh fruit	1 oz. apple = 10 calories
	1 oz. orange = 8 calories
	1 oz. banana = 13 calories
with cornflakes	¾ oz. = 78 calories
Fresh orange segments	1 oz. = 10 calories
Grilled kipper	1 oz. = 31 calories
Tomato juice	1 oz. = 7 calories
Poached egg	1 standard egg = 46 calories per oz.
Lemon juice	
Grilled sausage	1 oz. = 87 calories
and tomato	
Stewed prunes	1 oz. = 19 calories
Scrambled egg	
Orange juice	
Smoked haddock	1 oz. = 18 calories
1 apple	
Baked egg	
1 Pear	1 oz. = 11 calories
Tomatoes and mushroom kebab	

This selection of soups and hors d'oeuvres are specially created for slimmers, but they are also ideal appetizers that will delight your family and guests.

Serve them too for a light lunch with some cheese and fresh fruit to follow.

Consommé Madrilène

1 lb. tomatoes; 1 onion; 2 sticks celery; 1 pint water; 4 peppercorns; 1 bay leaf; 10½ oz. can consommé; salt. Quarter the tomatoes, peel and slice onion and chop the celery. Put the vegetables into a saucepan with the water, peppercorns and bay leaf. Bring to the boil and simmer for 20 minutes. Strain the soup and press the vegetables through the sieve. Return to the pan and add consommé and salt to taste. Reheat before serving.
Serves 4 at 70 calories per person.

Chicken and Herb Soup

2 pints water; 2 chicken stock cubes; 1 onion; 1 teasp. dried tarragon; salt and pepper; ½ teasp. grated lemon rind; 2 tbsp. chopped chives.
Put the water and stock cubes into a saucepan and bring to the boil. Chop the onion and add to the stock with tarragon, salt, pepper and lemon rind. Simmer for 5 minutes. Strain before serving. Garnish with chopped chives.
Serves 4 at 11 calories per person.

Iced Tomato Soup

1 lb. ripe tomatoes; 1 small green pepper; 1 onion; 1 clove garlic; salt and pepper; ½ pint (approx.) cold water.
Dip tomatoes into boiling water and remove the skin.

Chop the tomatoes and place in a basin. Halve green pepper and remove core and seeds, slice very thinly. Peel and finely chop onion and crush garlic. Add all these to the tomatoes with salt and pepper to taste. Stir in enough cold water to thin the soup slightly. Leave in refrigerator for at least an hour until really cold.
Serves 3 at 35 calories per person.

Watercress Soup

2 bunches watercress; 1½ pints water; 2 chicken stock cubes; 1 oz. dried low-fat milk; salt and pepper; pinch nutmeg.

Wash watercress in cold, salted water. Place in a saucepan with water and stock cubes. Bring to the boil and simmer for 15 minutes. Sieve or put through an electric blender. Return to the pan and add low-fat milk powder, salt and pepper, and nutmeg. Bring to the boil and serve. If liked, this soup can be served cold; leave to cool and chill before serving.
Serves 3 at 38 calories per person.

Asparagus Soup

1 small onion; 1 pint water; 15 oz. can asparagus spears; 1 chicken stock cube; salt and pepper; garlic salt.

Peel and chop the onion and boil in water until soft. Drain the asparagus and add liquor to the onion. Stir in stock cube. Chop the asparagus, reserving a few of the tips for garnish. Add chopped asparagus to the pan, bring to the boil and simmer for 5 minutes. Put the soup mixture through a sieve, or if available, blend in an electric blender. Return to the pan and add salt and pepper and garlic salt to taste, heat before serving. Garnish with the asparagus tips.
Serves 4 at 15 calories per person.

Brown Onion Soup

1 lb. onions; $\frac{1}{2}$ oz. butter or margarine; 2 pints water;
2 beef stock cubes; salt and pepper.

Peel and chop onions and gently fry in butter or margarine
until brown. Stir in water, stock cubes, salt and pepper to
taste. Bring to the boil, then reduce heat and simmer for
20 minutes until onions are soft.

Serves 4 at 59 calories per person.

Carrot and Celery Broth

1 lb. carrots; 4 sticks celery; 1 small onion; 2 pints
water; 2 beef stock cubes; pinch nutmeg; salt and
pepper; chopped parsley.

Peel and slice carrots, scrape celery and cut into slices.
Peel and slice onion. Put the vegetables into a saucepan
with water and stock cubes. Bring to the boil, cover, then
simmer for 1 hour. Put the soup through a sieve or electric
blender, and return to the pan. Stir in pinch nutmeg, salt
and pepper to taste and serve garnished with chopped
parsley.

Serves 4 at 39 calories per person.

Tomato and Leek Soup

1 lb. tomatoes; $\frac{1}{2}$ lb. leeks; 2 pints water; 2 beef stock
cubes; $\frac{1}{2}$ teasp. sugar; salt and pepper; 5 oz. carton
soured cream.

Quarter the tomatoes, wash the leeks well and slice.
Put both of these into a saucepan and add water and stock
cubes. Bring to the boil, cover the pan, then simmer for
$\frac{3}{4}$ hour. Put the soup through a sieve, return to the pan
and add sugar, salt and pepper to taste. Reheat and
serve with a spoonful of soured cream on top.

Serves 4 at 107 calories per person.

Cucumber Soup

1 cucumber; 1 onion; 1½ pints water; salt and pepper;
1 chicken stock cube; 5 oz. carton plain yogurt; few
drops green colouring, optional.

Remove skin from cucumber and cut into slices. Peel
and chop onion. Put these in a saucepan with the water,
salt, pepper and stock cube. Bring to the boil and simmer
for 20 minutes. Sieve the soup or put through an electric
blender. Leave to cool, then beat in the yogurt and green
colouring, if used. Chill before serving.
Serves 4 at 82 calories per person.

Avocado and Crab Cocktail

2 ripe avocado pears; 3¼ oz. can crab meat; 1 tbsp.
vinegar; 1–2 drops liquid sweetener; salt and pepper.

Halve pears and remove the stones. Drain crab meat and
flake. Mix vinegar with sweetener, salt and pepper and
pour over the crab meat. Pile the mixture into the avocado pears and garnish with watercress or parsley.
Serves 4 at 80 calories per person.

Avocado and Lemon Mousse

2 ripe avocado pears; juice 1 lemon; ½ teasp. Worcestershire sauce; 1–2 drops liquid sweetener; salt and pepper.

Halve pears, remove stones and scoop the flesh out into a
basin. Beat this with the lemon juice. Add rest of ingredients and pile the mixture into the shells. Garnish with a
piece of lemon.
Serves 4 at 53 calories per person.

Sea Food Special

1 large carton frozen cod steaks; 2 oz. peeled prawns;
2 sticks celery; 2 tbsp. tomato purée; juice 1 lemon;
2 teasp. chopped parsley; salt, paprika pepper.

45

Poach cod steaks in a little water for 10 minutes until cooked (if still frozen, they may take a little longer). Drain, leave to cool, then flake. Chop celery, and gently mix with the cod. Put into individual glasses and arrange prawns on top. Make sauce by mixing tomato purée, lemon juice, parsley with salt and paprika, to taste. Spoon over the fish.
Serves 4 at 100 calories per person.

Chicken Liver Pâté

8 oz. chicken livers; 1 small onion; 1 oz. butter; 2 tbsp. white wine; ⅛ teasp. ground cloves; ⅛ teasp. ground nutmeg; pinch salt and pepper.
Cook the chicken livers and onion in salted water for about 15 minutes, drain well. Put through a mincer, or chop very finely. Slightly melt the butter, and mix with wine, cloves, nutmeg, salt and pepper and stir this into the liver and onion. Spoon into a basin and leave in refrigerator to chill.
Serves 4 at 145 calories per person.

MAIN MEALS

These recipes are for the main meal of the day – whether you have it at lunch-time or in the evening is a matter of choice, but two should not be chosen in the same day if you are limiting the total calories to the number suggested in the introduction.

Savoury Herb Hamburgers

1 small onion; ¾ lb. minced beef; ½ teasp. mixed herbs; 1 teasp. chopped parsley; pinch garlic salt; salt and pepper; 1 tbsp. cold water; ½ oz. butter.
Peel and finely chop the onion and mix with the minced steak. Stir in herbs, parsley, garlic salt, salt and pepper

to taste. Add the water and mix well. Divide the mixture into small pieces and roll each piece into a ball and flatten slightly. Place the hamburgers in the grill pan and dot with butter. Cook under medium heat for about 5 minutes each side.

Serves 4 at 186 calories per person.

Lamb Hot Pot

1½ lb. scrag end lamb; 2 onions; 4 sticks celery; ½ lb. carrots; salt and pepper; 1 pint stock or water. Cut the meat into pieces, peel and slice onion, wash and chop celery and scrape and slice carrots. Place the ingredients in an ovenproof dish and season with salt and pepper. Pour over the stock or water. Cover the dish and cook in a moderate oven. Mark 4, 350° F. for 1½–2 hours until meat is tender.

Serves 4 at 390 calories per person.

Slimmers' Boeuf Stroganoff

1 lb. rump steak; 2 small onions; 3 tbsp. tomato purée; ⅛ pint red wine; ¼ pint water; 1 teasp. paprika pepper; salt; 5 oz. carton soured cream. Remove any fat from the meat and cut into thin strips. Peel and chop the onions. Place meat in a pan and fry quickly, stirring, until the meat is lightly browned. Add the onions, tomato purée, wine, water, paprika pepper and salt to taste. Cover the pan and simmer for ¾ hour. Just before serving, stir in the soured cream.

Serves 4 at 320 calories per person.

Lamb and Tomato Casserole

2 onions; 4 loin of lamb chops (4 oz. each); salt and pepper; 1 tbsp. chopped parsley; ½ lb. tomatoes; ½ pint water. Peel and slice the onions and place in a casserole. Re

excess fat from the chops and put on top of the onions.
Sprinkle with salt and pepper and the chopped parsley.
Slice tomatoes and arrange over the chops. Pour in the
water and cover the casserole. Cook at Mark 3, 325° F. for
1–1½ hours.
Serves 4 at 102 calories per person.

Liver and Onion Casserole

½ lb. onions; ¾ lb. lamb's liver; 2 sticks celery; ½ lb.
carrots; ½ pint water; 1 meat stock cube.

Peel and slice onions and place in an ovenproof casserole.
Cut the liver into serving size pieces and place on top of
the onions. Slice the celery and peel and slice carrots.
Place these on top of the liver. Pour over the stock made
with water and stock cube and cover casserole with a
well-fitting lid. Cook in a slow oven, Mark 2, 300° F. for
2–2½ hours until vegetables are tender.
Serves 4 at 152 calories per person.

Tomato-stuffed Meat Balls

1 lb. lean minced beef; 4 tbsp. dried non-fat milk;
1 teasp. dried mustard; pinch garlic salt; pinch mixed
herbs; ⅛ teasp. ground nutmeg; salt and pepper;
2 tbsp. water; 2 oz. cheese; 14 oz. can tomatoes.

Mix minced steak with the milk powder, mustard, garlic
salt, mixed herbs, nutmeg and salt and pepper to taste.
Add the water and mix well. Divide into 12 equal pieces
and shape into flat round cakes. Cut the cheese into cubes
and place one in the centre of each meat cake. Mould steak
around to form a ball. Place tomatoes in a saucepan and
bring to the boil. Add the meat balls, cover the pan and
simmer gently for 35–40 minutes.
Serves 4 at 328 calories per person.

Kidney Ragoût

1 lb. ox kidneys; ½ oz. butter; 14 oz. can tomatoes;
2 teasp. dried onion flakes; salt and pepper; 1 small
green pepper.

Remove any skin and fat from the kidney and cut into
small pieces. Fry the kidney gently in the butter until
just brown. Stir in the tomatoes, onion flakes, salt and
pepper to taste and cook gently for 10 minutes. Halve the
pepper, remove seeds and slice. Add this to the ragoût
and cook for a further 15 minutes.
Serves 4 at 180 calories per person.

Mexican Chicken

4 (6 oz.) chicken quarters; 1 oz. butter; 1 onion;
1 clove garlic; 6 oz. can red peppers; ⅛ teasp. salt;
¼ teasp. chilli powder; ¾ pint water; 1 chicken stock
cube.

Remove skin from the chicken and fry in butter until
golden brown, then place in an ovenproof dish. Peel and
slice onion and crush the garlic. Drain red peppers, slice
and add to the chicken with the onion and garlic. Sprinkle
in the salt and chilli powder and pour in the chicken
stock made with water and the stock cube. Cover the
dish and cook at Mark 4, 350° F. for 1½ hours.
Serves 4 at 308 calories per person.

Apple and Chicken Casserole

1 onion; ¼ lb. cooking apples; 2 oz. crumbs made
from starch-reduced bread; ½ teasp. mixed herbs;
pinch salt and pepper; ½ pint cider; 2½ lb. roasting
chicken.

Chop the onion, peel, core and chop the apples and mix
with breadcrumbs, mixed herbs, salt and pepper and add
a little of the cider to make a stiff mixture. Stuff the
chicken with this and place in a deep ovenproof casserole.

Pour remaining cider around the chicken and cover the dish with a lid or piece of foil. Cook in a moderate oven, Mark 4, 350° F. for 2 hours until chicken is tender
Serves 4 at 482 calories per person.

Chicken à l'Orange

1 onion; 1 oz. butter; 4 (6 oz.) chicken quarters; 2 sticks celery; grated rind of 1 and juice of 2 oranges; 1 tbsp. chopped parsley; 1 oz. green olives.

Chop the onion and fry in butter until beginning to brown. Add the chicken and fry on both sides for a few minutes. Put chicken and onion into an ovenproof casserole. Slice celery and add to the chicken. Mix orange rind, juice, chopped parsley and olives and pour over the chicken. Cover the casserole and cook at Mark 4, 350° F. for about 1 hour until chicken is tender.
Serves 4 at 312 calories per person.

Curried Chicken

Juice 1 lemon; 2 tbsp. curry powder; 4 (6 oz.) chicken quarters; 1 oz. butter.

Mix lemon juice and curry powder together and spread the mixture over the chicken. Melt the butter in a grill pan and place the chicken in pan, meat side down. Cook for 10 minutes under medium heat then turn the chicken. Baste frequently with the sauce in the pan. Cook for a further 25 minutes, turning once or twice. Serve with the sauce poured over the chicken.
Serves 4 at 298 calories per person.

Salmon Mousse

½ oz. powdered gelatin; ¼ pint boiling water; 8 oz. can salmon; 1 lb. cottage cheese; salt and pepper; juice ½ lemon.

Dissolve gelatin in the boiling water. Drain salmon and

remove skin and bones. Flake the fish into a basin and mix in cottage cheese, salt and pepper to taste and the lemon juice. Stir in dissolved gelatin and mix well. Pour into a 1-pint soufflé dish and leave to set.
Serves 4 at 146 calories per person.

Cheese-topped Scallops

8 scallops; ½ pint milk; 2 oz. starch reduced-bread-crumbs; 2 oz. grated cheese; ½ teasp. made mustard; salt and pepper.

Remove scallops from shells and cut each into 4. Simmer in the milk for 5 minutes. Meanwhile, wash and lightly butter the shells. Drain scallops, reserve the milk, and place in the shells. Mix milk with crumbs, half of the cheese, mustard, salt and pepper. Cook over the scallops. Sprinkle remainder of the cheese over the top. Place under a medium grill until golden brown on top.
Serves 4 at 248 calories per person.

Prawns with Cucumber Cheese

1 small cucumber; 4 oz. cottage cheese; salt and pepper; pinch garlic salt; 1 tbsp. vinegar; 8 oz. prawns; few lettuce leaves; 2 tomatoes.

Peel and dice cucumber, sprinkle with a little salt and leave in a cool place for ½ hour. Drain off liquid and mix cucumber with cottage cheese, garlic salt, pepper and vinegar. Arrange the prawns on a bed of lettuce, quarter the tomatoes and place around the sides. Spoon the cucumber cheese on top.
Serves 2 at 215 calories per person.

Plaice and Watercress Sauce

1 lb. plaice fillets; 1 bunch watercress; 1 oz. butter; 1 oz. flour; 2 oz. dried non-fat milk; ¾ pint water; salt and pepper; cayenne pepper; 2 tomatoes.

51

Wash plaice fillets and poach for 5 minutes in gently boiling water. Wash watercress, place in pan, cover with cold water and bring to the boil. Cook for 2 minutes, drain and chop very finely. Melt butter, add flour and cook for 1 minute. Mix milk powder with water and add to flour and butter, stirring continuously. Add watercress, seasoning, a dash of cayenne pepper and heat gently. Pour sauce over hot fish and garnish with thin slices of tomato.

Serves 4 at 240 calories per person.

Sole Duglère

1 onion; ½ lb. tomatoes; 1 crushed clove garlic, optional; salt; pepper; ¼ teasp. sugar; 1 tbsp. chopped parsley; 1 lb. fillets of sole; lemon juice.

Peel and chop the onion, skin and slice tomatoes. Put both in a saucepan and cook gently until onion is almost soft. Add garlic, if used, salt, pepper, sugar and parsley and pour into an ovenproof dish. Skin the fish and sprinkle with a little lemon juice. Roll up and place on top of the tomato mixture. Cover the dish and cook at Mark 5, 375° F. for 30–40 minutes.

Serves 4 at 113 calories per person.

Prawn Américaine

¼ lb. onions; ½ lb. tomatoes; 2–3 tbsp. dry white wine; salt; cayenne pepper; ½ lb. peeled prawns.

Peel and finely chop the onions. Skin and slice tomatoes. Place these in a saucepan with the wine and cook gently, with the lid on, for 20 minutes. Add salt, cayenne pepper to taste and stir in the prawns. Cook for a further 10 minutes.

Serves 2 at 160 calories per person.

Nutritious, light meals that are designed as a midday snack, supper or packed lunch, and some of the salads make ideal accompaniments to your main meal, providing you choose those low in calories!

Stuffed Cabbage

8 large cabbage leaves; 12 oz. lean minced beef; 4 tbsp. dried non-fat milk; 1 level tbsp. grated onion; ½ level teasp. mixed herbs; 1 teasp. Worcester sauce; salt and pepper; 14 oz. can tomato juice; 1 teasp. lemon juice.

Cover cabbage leaves with boiling water (salted) for 5 minutes. Drain and cut away hard stems. Mix together minced beef, dried non-fat milk, onion, herbs, Worcester sauce and salt and pepper to taste. Spoon equal amounts of mixture on to centres of cabbage leaves. Fold edges of leaves over filling, parcel fashion. Transfer to ovenproof dish and if necessary, secure with wooden cocktail sticks. Pour tomato juice into dish then sprinkle with lemon juice and salt and pepper. Cover. Cook just above centre of oven, Mark 4, 350° F. for 1 hour.
Serves 4 at 261 calories per person.

Cheese-stuffed Marrow

½ medium-sized marrow; ½ oz. porridge oats; 2 oz. grated Cheddar cheese; 1 egg yolk; 1 tbsp. dried non-fat milk; 2 tbsp. cold water; seasoning to taste.

Peel marrow and scoop out seeds with a spoon. Mix together oats with cheese, then bind with egg yolk and milk powder. Mix in the water. Season to taste with salt and pepper and spoon into marrow shell. Wrap completely in foil, stand in a large saucepan and cover with boiling water. Cover saucepan with lid and simmer for 40 minutes.

53

Unwrap marrow and cut into slices. Serve hot with grilled or baked tomatoes.
Serves 3 at 154 calories per person.

Pepper Omelette

2 eggs; 2 tbsp. water; pinch paprika pepper; $\frac{1}{4}$ oz. butter; 1 canned red pepper.

Lightly beat the eggs, water, salt and paprika pepper. Heat butter in an omelette or small frying-pan. Pour in eggs and cook quickly. Lift the edges with a fork or palette knife so that the uncooked egg runs underneath. Chop the red pepper and place on top of the omelette. When the eggs are set, fold over and serve.
Serves 1 at 286 calories.

Leeks au Gratin

6 leeks (1 lb. after trimming); 4 level tbsp. dried non-fat milk; 4 oz. grated cheese; 2 eggs; paprika pepper.

Trim leeks and cut into half lengthwise. Wash thoroughly and cut into 2 in. lengths. Cook in boiling salted water for 20 minutes. Drain. Return pan of leeks to low heat and stir in milk powder, 4 oz. of the cheese and beaten eggs. Mix well and place in an ovenproof dish. Sprinkle remaining cheese on top and a little paprika pepper. Place in the oven at Mark 5, 375° F. for 20 minutes until golden brown.
Serves 3 at 342 calories per person.

Savoury Tomatoes

4 large (or 8 small) tomatoes; 2 oz. cooked lean ham; few chives (or little grated onion); 2 oz. grated cheese; salt and pepper.

Slice tops off the tomatoes and scoop flesh into a basin. Chop the ham and mix with tomato flesh. Add chopped chives, grated cheese, salt and pepper, and mix well.

Spoon the mixture back into the tomatoes. Serve cold, or if liked, place in an ovenproof dish and bake at Mark 4, 350° F. for 30 minutes until hot through.
Serves 4 at 101 calories per person.

Salad Medley

6 spring onions; 1 bunch radishes; 2 carrots; ½ small cucumber; 5 oz. carton soured cream; juice ½ lemon; ¼ teasp. paprika pepper; salt.
Prepare vegetables and cut into small pieces. Mix soured cream with lemon juice, paprika pepper and salt to taste. Stir vegetables into the dressing and chill. Serve with lettuce.
Serves 2 at 272 calories per person.

Tuna and Egg Salad

7 oz. can tuna fish; 2 hard-boiled eggs; 1 small onion; 4 tbsp. soured cream; 2 teasp. tomato ketchup; salt and pepper.
Drain tuna fish and flake. Shell eggs and cut into quarters. Peel and slice the onion. Arrange these on plates. Mix soured cream with tomato ketchup, salt and pepper and spoon over the salad.
Serves 2 at 316 calories per person.

Cheese and Pineapple Salad

4 oz. Cheddar cheese; small fresh pineapple or 8½ oz. can slices; 2 oz. cottage cheese; *To garnish:* watercress.
Cut the cheese into slices, peel fresh pineapple, remove core and cut into slices (or drain canned pineapple). Place cheese on top of pineapple slices and top with a spoonful of cottage cheese. Garnish with watercress.
Serves 2 at 286 calories per person.

Tomato and Mushroom Salad

1 lb. tomatoes; ½ lb. mushrooms; 2 teasp. grated onion; ¼ pint tomato juice; 1 teasp. lemon juice; 1 teasp. Worcestershire sauce; salt and pepper.

Peel and slice tomatoes, wipe and slice mushrooms. Place these in a basin with grated onion sprinkled over the top. Mix tomato juice with lemon juice, Worcestershire sauce, salt and pepper to taste. Pour over the salad and chill before serving.

Serves 4 at 33 calories per person.

Cheese, Apple and Celery Salad

½ lb. Cheddar cheese; ½ lb. crisp eating apples; lemon juice; 4 sticks celery; 4 oz. cottage cheese.

Cut cheese into cubes, peel and slice apples and dip in lemon juice, chop celery. Mix these in a basin and serve topped with cottage cheese.

Serves 4 at 302 calories per person.

Tossed Red Cabbage

½ lb. red cabbage; 3 sticks celery; 1 small cauliflower; 1 onion; 2 tbsp. vinegar; ¼ pint tomato juice; 1 teasp. made mustard; salt; pepper; liquid sugar substitute.

Wash and slice cabbage and celery. Remove leaves and stalks from cauliflower and divide into small flowerets. Mix together in a basin. Peel and thinly slice onion, separate into rings and arrange on top of the salad. Mix vinegar, tomato juice, mustard, salt, pepper and sugar substitute to taste and pour over the salad.

Serves 4 at 62 calories per person.

Tomato and Chicken Deckers

8 tomatoes; 2 hard-boiled eggs; 4 oz. cold cooked chicken; salt and pepper; ¼ teasp. curry powder; juice ½ lemon;

To serve: 8 stuffed olives; lettuce.

Cut tomatoes across into 3 slices. Mash hard-boiled eggs and mix with finely chopped chicken. Season to taste with salt, pepper and add curry powder and mix to a soft consistency with lemon juice. Sandwich the tomato slices with the egg and chicken mixture. Put a cocktail stick through each one and serve tomatoes on a bed of lettuce. Stick an olive on top of each.
Serves 4 at 105 calories per person.

Coleslaw

1 lb. cabbage; ½ lb. carrots; 1 small onion; 3 sticks celery; 3 tbsp. wine vinegar; ¼ teasp. dry mustard; salt and pepper; liquid sugar substitute.
Wash vegetables, prepare and cut into small slices. Mix together and place in a basin. Mix vinegar, mustard, salt, pepper and liquid sugar substitute to taste. Stir dressing into the salad and mix well.
Serves 4 at 52 calories per person.

Spanish Salad

1 green pepper; 2 sticks celery; 1 small onion; few green olives; 4–6 leaves lettuce; 2 tbsp. vinegar; salt and pepper; 1 tbsp. chopped parsley.
Halve the pepper, remove the seeds and slice. Peel and slice onion and chop the celery. Mix these together with the olives and before serving shred the lettuce, and mix in. Mix vinegar, salt, pepper and chopped parsley and pour over the salad.
Serves 2 at 30 calories per person.

Crab and Celery Salad

3¼ oz. can crab meat; 6 sticks celery; 2 tbsp. vinegar; 2 tbsp. tomato juice; 1 teasp. chopped parsley; 1–2 drops liquid sugar substitute; 1 basket mustard and cress.

Drain crab, flake, and remove any slivers of bones. Chop celery and mix with the crab. Mix rest of ingredients together except mustard and cress, and pour over the salad. Serve topped with the mustard and cress.
Serves 2 at 76 calories per person.

PUDDINGS

Puddings and sweets are usually associated with rich, creamy or stodgy foods which are fattening, so slimmers will always avoid them. As most people like something sweet to finish a meal, the desserts in this section are for you – sweet, but with few calories and with lots of fruit which is good for you.

Apricot Purée

4 oz. dried apricots; grated rind ½ lemon; liquid sugar substitute; 5 oz. plain yogurt.

Soak apricots overnight in cold water. Place apricots and water in a saucepan with lemon rind and cook until soft. Put through a sieve or electric blender. Add sugar substitute to taste and leave to cool. Before serving, stir in the yogurt.
Serves 4 at 71 calories per person.

Pineapple Cheese

1 lb. cottage cheese; grated rind and juice 1 lemon; 8 oz. can pineapple pieces; ½ oz. gelatin; liquid sugar substitute; 2 eggs.

Sieve the cottage cheese and stir in lemon rind and juice. Drain pineapple and place liquid in a basin over a pan of boiling water, add gelatin and stir until dissolved. Separate eggs and add yolks to gelatin mixture, stir over heat

until creamy. Cool slightly then pour into the cottage cheese. Stir pineapple into the mixture. Beat the egg whites and fold into the cottage cheese. Spoon into a serving dish and leave to set.
Serves 6 at 150 calories per person.

Spiced Oranges

3 oranges; ½ pint water; ½ teasp. ground cinnamon; ⅛ teasp. nutmeg; liquid sugar substitute.
Peel the oranges and remove all the pith. Cut fruit into slices. Place water and spices into a saucepan with 1–2 drops sugar substitute. Bring to the boil then add orange slices. Simmer for 3 minutes, pour into a dish and leave to cool.
Serves 4 at 40 calories per person.

Raspberry Sorbet

8 oz. packet frozen raspberries; cold water (see method); juice 1 lemon; liquid sugar substitute; 1 egg white.
When raspberries are thawed, mash with a fork to make a purée. Add sufficient water to make ¾ pint. Stir in lemon juice and sugar substitute to taste. Beat egg white until stiff and fold into the raspberry mixture. Spoon into ice trays and place in the frozen food compartment of the refrigerator for about an hour. Stir well then freeze until firm.
Serves 4 at 18 calories per person.

Apple Snow

1 lb. cooking apples; liquid sugar substitute; ½ teasp. grated lemon rind; 1 egg white.
Peel and slice apples and cook in a little water until soft. Drain off any excess liquid and put apples through a sieve or electric blender. Add sugar substitute to taste, and

stir in grated lemon rind and leave to cool. Beat egg white and fold into the apples before serving.
Serves 4 at 44 calories per person.

Rhubarb and Ginger Pudding

1 lb. rhubarb; liquid sugar substitute; 2 tbsp. lemon juice; 2 oz. white starch-reduced breadcrumbs; 1 teasp. ground ginger; ½ oz. butter.

Wash rhubarb and cut into pieces. Place in an ovenproof pie-dish and sprinkle over 2–3 drops sugar substitute and lemon juice. Mix breadcrumbs with ginger and spoon over the fruit. Put the butter in small pieces over the top. Bake at Mark 4, 350° F. for 30–40 minutes until the fruit is soft (test with a pointed knife) and top is golden.
Serves 4 at 71 calories per person.

Fruit Jelly

1 packet orange or lemon jelly; 1 orange; 1 apple; ¼ lb. grapes; 2 oz. cherries.

Make up jelly with ¾ pint of water and leave until just cool and almost set. Prepare the fruit and cut into pieces. Stir the fruit into the jelly, spoon into a serving dish and leave in a cool place to set.
Serves 6 at 95 calories per person

Orange Jelly

¼ pint water; ½ oz. gelatin; 1 can frozen orange juice; water (see method); juice ½ lemon; liquid sugar substitute.

Bring the water to the boil, remove from heat and stir in gelatin to dissolve. Mix thawed orange juice with cold water to make ¾ pint, add lemon juice and stir into the gelatin. Add liquid sugar substitute to taste. Pour into a serving dish or wetted mould and leave in a cool place to set.
Serves 4 at 18 calories per person.

Pear Meringue

4 fresh pears; juice ½ lemon; 2 egg whites; liquid sugar substitute.

Peel pears, halve and remove core, poach in a little water and lemon juice until soft. Drain and place in an oven-proof dish. Beat the egg whites until stiff add 1–2 drops of liquid sugar substitute. Spoon the meringue over the pears and place in the oven at Mark 3, 325° F. for about 10 minutes or until meringue is golden brown.
Serves 4 at 51 calories per person.

Coffee Creams

¼ pint strong coffee; ½ oz. gelatin; liquid sugar substitute; 10 oz. can Danish cream; 1 dessertsp. brandy.

Bring the coffee to boiling point, sprinkle in the gelatin and stir until dissolved. Pour into a basin and stir in the cream. Leave to cool, but not set, add the brandy then whisk until fluffy. Pour into individual glasses and leave in a cool place to set.
Serves 4 at 102 calories per person.

INDEX

63

11/1974

The Calorie Counter